Boston Red Sox Autograp[h]

Throw The Ball Publishing

Printed in the United States of America

Copyright © 2011 by Richard Brown

All rights reserved. No part of this publication may be reproduced, stored in a retrieval system, or transmitted in any form or by any means, electronic, mechanical, recording, or otherwise, without the prior written permission of the author.

Cataloging-in-Publication Data is available from the Library of Congress.

Boston Red Sox Autograph Book

Introduction

THE BOSTON RED SOX program is simply the best. No ifs, buts or doubts about it.

The facilities, the coaches, players, administrative support and fans are among the finest anywhere. But it's been a long journey – it didn't happen overnight. It was a gradual process with ups and downs. For sure, the journey has included a number of outstanding players and coaches.

The intent of this book is to help you create your own memories of some of the finest players and the coaches who have played such a significant role in helping make the Boston Red Sox the best.

Red Sox Nation, use this book to get your players and coaches Autographs and keep it as a keepsake.

It's great to be the Red Sox!

Autographs

Autographs

Autographs

Autographs

Autographs

Autographs

Autographs

Autographs

Autographs

Autographs

Autographs

Autographs

Autographs

Autographs

Autographs

Autographs

Autographs

Autographs

Autographs

Autographs

Autographs

Made in the USA
Monee, IL
09 March 2025

13736962R00015